HABITAT SURVIVAL

RIVERS

Melanie Waldron

Chicago, Illinois

www.capstonepub.com
Visit our website to find out
more information about
Heinemann-Raintree books.

To order:
☎ Phone 800-747-4992
🖥 Visit www.capstonepub.com
to browse our catalog and order online.

© 2013 Raintree
an imprint of Capstone Global Library, LLC
Chicago, Illinois

Edited by Nancy Dickmann, Kristen Kowalkowski,
and Claire Throp
Designed by Philippa Jenkins
Original illustrations © Capstone Global Library Ltd
2013
Illustrations by Jeff Edwards, and Kamae Design
Picture research by Tracy Cummins
Originated by Capstone Global Library Ltd
Printed and bound by in China by CTPS

16 15 14 13 12
10 9 8 7 6 5 4 3 2 1

Library of Congress Cataloging-in-Publication Data
Waldron, Melanie.
  Rivers / Melanie Waldron.
    p. cm.—(Habitat survival)
  Includes bibliographical references and index.
  ISBN 978-1-4109-4600-3 (hb)—ISBN 978-1-4109-
4609-6 (pb) 1. Rivers—Juvenile literature. I. Title.
  GB1203.8.W35 2012
  577.6'4—dc23   2012000244

Acknowledgments
We would like to thank the following for permission
to reproduce photographs: Alamy pp. 24
(© Excitations), 25 (© Neil Denham), 26 (© Paul
Glendell); Biosphoto p. 19 (Pierre Huguet); Corbis
p. 22 (© Les Stone/Sygma); FLPA pp. 7 (Willem
Kolvoort/FN), 9 (David Hosking), 10 (Michael Weber/
Imagebroker), 12 (Scott Linstead/Minden Pictures),
14 (Tim Fitzharris/Minden Pictures); Getty Images
p. 27 (Joel Sartore); National Geographic p. 5 (Joe
Petersburger); Nature Picture Library p. 11 (Doug
Perrine); Shutterstock pp. 6 (© Yuriy Kulyk), 13
(© Ryan M. Bolton), 16 (© David P. Lewis), 17
(© Lorraine Logan), 18 (© A.S. Zain), 20 (© Igor
Jandric), 21 (© Mike Norton); Superstock pp. 8
(© Pixtal Images), 29 (© Ambient Images Inc/Peter
Bennett).

Cover photograph of a red swamp crayfish in the
Mijares River, Spain, reproduced with permission of
Photolibrary/Javier Tajuelo.

Contents

Some words are shown in bold, **like this**. You can find out what they mean by looking in the glossary.

A Watery World

There are rivers of many different sizes all over the world. They are all part of Earth's water cycle. This is the continuous movement of water around Earth. The water cycle includes rivers, oceans, clouds, rain, snow, and ice.

Rivers form when water collects together and runs in a **channel**. Channels flow downhill, joining up with other channels to become larger and larger. Eventually, rivers meet the sea.

This diagram shows how rivers are part of the water cycle.

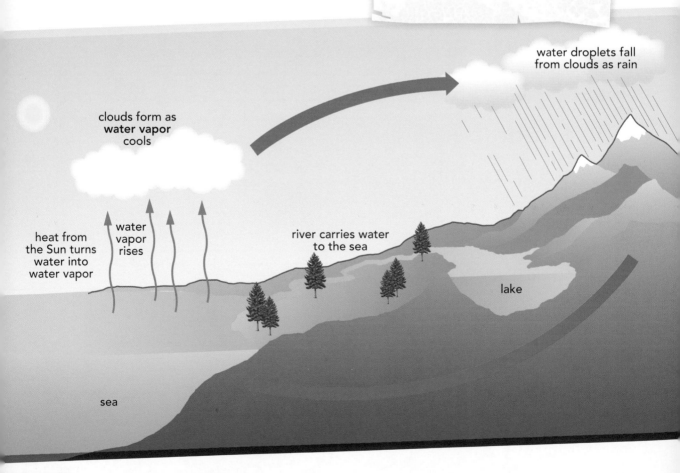

water droplets fall from clouds as rain

clouds form as **water vapor** cools

heat from the Sun turns water into water vapor

water vapor rises

river carries water to the sea

lake

sea

Kingfishers are beautiful birds that live near rivers. They are skilled at catching fish.

Changing the land

As rivers run over land, the water can pick up and move bits of soil, plants, and rock. Over time, rivers can carve out great channels through the landscape. This is called **erosion**. Small rivers can carry only very small pieces of **sediment**. Large, powerful rivers can carry rocks and boulders.

River records

Here are some of the world's biggest rivers:

Longest river	Nile River (Africa)	4,132 miles (6,650 kilometers) long
Largest volume (amount) of water	Amazon River (South America)	The river contains about one-fifth of the world's freshwater.
Deepest river	Congo River (Africa)	640 feet (195 meters)

How Do Plants Live Underwater?

Many different kinds of plants grow along the sides of rivers. Some also grow along riverbeds. The big challenge for plants is staying where they are and not being swept downstream. They do this by attaching their roots to bits of **sediment** on the riverbed. Many plants also have leaves with very fine tassels, like fingers. This prevents the water from dragging on them so much.

Water lily pads float on the surface of a river. This means they can capture sunlight to make food.

Trapped!

Bladderwort grows in water. It has bright yellow flowers. But insects, beware! It also has little traps that float on the surface, waiting to suck in any insect that comes too close.

Making food

Plants need sunlight to make food for themselves. Plants growing under the water will get less sunlight because the water blocks some of it. Some plants have **adapted** to this by having leaves that float on the surface. Others have leaves that stick up above the surface.

Plants also need gases such as **carbon dioxide** and **oxygen**. They can **absorb** this from clean water, which contains these gases. They can also absorb chemicals called **nutrients** from water, to help them grow.

How Do Animals Live Underwater?

All animals need **oxygen** to live, even animals living in rivers. Clean river water contains oxygen, so animals can use this. Some, like most fish, have **gills**. These are tiny, feathery body parts that **absorb** oxygen. Others, such as leeches, absorb oxygen straight through their skin.

Living on the move

River animals also have to cope with flowing water. Fish have long, narrow bodies that they point upstream, so the water flows around them. Some, such as brook trout, swim all the time to stay in one place. Others, like miller's-thumb, hide beneath stones on the riverbed.

Crayfish have gills underneath their smooth, sleek shells. They walk about on the riverbed to avoid the faster water above.

Catfish in tropical rivers have suckers in place of their front fins. They use these to cling onto rocks and plants.

Slow rivers

More animals can be found in slower rivers. There are usually more plants and more **sediment**, where some minibeasts live. Frogs and newts can lay their eggs in slow, shallow areas.

Living Around Rivers

Many different animals live on and around rivers. Rivers can provide them with food, water, and homes. Birds such as ducks and dippers are well **adapted** to river life. Torrent ducks go fishing in mountain rivers in South America. They wade into very fast-flowing water. Facing upstream, they use their stiff tail feathers to brace themselves against rocks.

River mammals

Rivers are also home to some **mammals**. Beavers can close their noses and ears to keep out the water. They use their broad tails and webbed feet to swim. Hippos have nostrils high up on their heads. This is so that they can still breathe while they rest and cool off in the water.

Herons have long, thin beaks that they use to pluck fish from the water.

Amazonian manatees live in the Amazon River in South America. They have lots of gas in their bodies to keep them afloat.

River walkers

Dippers are little birds that flap their wings to swim down to the bottom of rivers. There, they walk along the riverbed looking for tadpoles, little fish, and insect **larvae**.

River Hunters!

Many river animals have developed special ways of hunting and catching food. Animals that hunt other animals are called predators. The animals they hunt are called prey.

Take aim, fire!

Archerfish spit jets of water at insects flying above the river surface. The insects fall into the water, and the archerfish gobble them up.

Caddisfly **larvae** spin little nets to trap tiny animals as they float down the river. Giant water bugs grab hold of their prey with their strong front claws. They then inject **poison** into their prey, and suck out their insides.

Bait fishing

Alligator snapping turtles have a little red flap of skin inside their mouths. They sit on riverbeds, camouflaged against the bottom. They open their mouths and wiggle the flap. Any fish that comes to inspect it quickly gets snapped up by the turtle.

Finding prey

Pikes are patient predators that use **camouflage** to hunt. They hide among plants and then burst out to catch fish. They also like to eat ducklings, frogs, and newts. Barbel fish use feelers to detect their prey as they swim along the riverbed.

A Web of Life

All living things in a **habitat** are connected to each other. This is because all living things need **energy** to survive. Plants need sunlight to make food for themselves. Some animals eat plants to get their energy. Some animals eat other animals, and some eat both plants and animals.

The energy in a **food chain** passes from plant to animal to animal, and so on. In a river habitat, many different animals eat many different things. This means that food chains are connected to other food chains. A food web is made of lots of connecting food chains.

This otter is eating a fish. Both are part of a river food web.

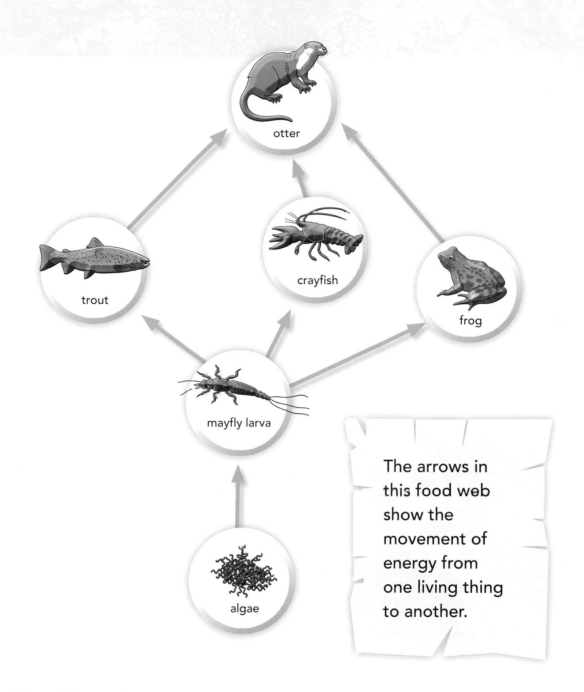

otter

crayfish

trout

frog

mayfly larva

algae

The arrows in this food web show the movement of energy from one living thing to another.

Breaking down waste

Decomposers are a very important part of river habitats. These animals eat the dead and rotting plant and animal waste that falls to the bottom of a river. Without decomposers, the waste would build up until the river was clogged with it. Some insect **larvae** and shellfish are decomposers.

Linked Together

In a river **habitat**, if one type of plant or animal becomes **extinct**, then there may be problems for other animals. For example, water snails eat plants called bulrush, and freshwater prawns eat the simple plants, called **algae**, that live on bulrush. If the bulrush is removed, both the water snails and the freshwater prawns will lose a source of food, and may die out. Then animals like crayfish, which eat water snails, and insects called water boatmen, which eat freshwater prawns, will die out, too.

New arrivals

Sometimes river habitats can be affected by a new plant or animal. For example, zebra mussels arrived in the United States in the 1980s. They came in large ships from Europe. They have now spread into many lakes and rivers. They are eating much of the food that **native** animals eat. Scientists are worried that the native animals may die out.

Zebra mussels might be a threat to the native animals of the United States.

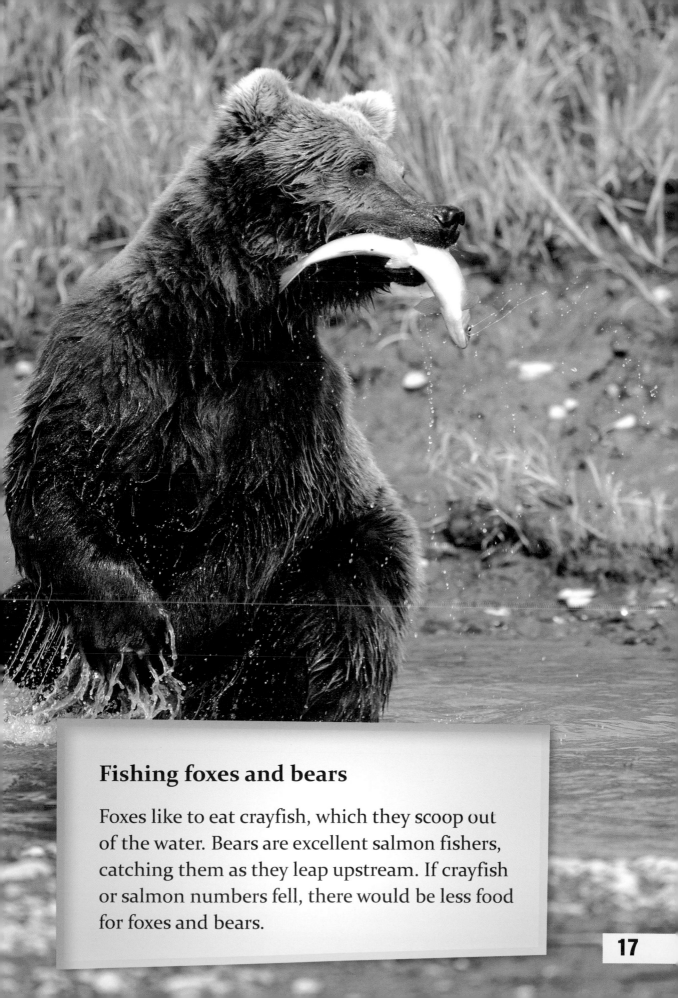

Fishing foxes and bears

Foxes like to eat crayfish, which they scoop out of the water. Bears are excellent salmon fishers, catching them as they leap upstream. If crayfish or salmon numbers fell, there would be less food for foxes and bears.

Living on Riverbanks

Many of the world's oldest towns and cities are close to rivers. Rivers provide water for people to drink and use. Before roads and railways, people traveled along rivers to other places.

In Borneo, people sell their goods from their boats at floating river markets.

Mississippi River

The Mississippi River is one of the world's longest rivers. People traveled along it in the 1800s to explore new areas. Today, there are many towns and cities along the river.

Fishing with cormorants

On the Li River in China, fishermen train birds called cormorants to catch fish for them. They tie a piece of string around the birds' necks. This prevents them from swallowing the fish. The birds are rewarded at the end with the smallest fish!

Making farmland

The land alongside rivers is often very good for growing things. This is because when rivers flood, they pour onto the land. Here, they can drop the **sediment** carried in the water. This makes the soil thick and rich—excellent for growing crops. In some countries, people build houses on stilts to keep dry during floods.

River Habitats at Risk

All over the world, river **habitats** are at risk. Different kinds of **pollution** are harming the plants and animals that live there. **Sewage** and **fertilizers** let tiny plants called **algae** grow in huge amounts. They use up the **oxygen** in the water, so few other plants and animals can survive. Chemicals can also be harmful to plants and animals.

Litter clogs up rivers and harms plants and animals.

Drying up

Water is a precious resource. Many rivers are affected by **irrigation**. This is when river water is used to water farmland. Some industries take river water to use in factories. Rivers can also dry up naturally. This can happen during droughts, when there is no rainfall to refill the rivers. When rivers lose water, plants and animals lose areas of habitat.

Not so Grande

The Rio Grande, in the southwest United States, is drying up. There are many large farms along its banks. They take out huge amounts of water for irrigation. This is causing fish and other river animals to die out.

Reshaping Rivers

Most rivers around the world have been changed in some way by humans. Many have been straightened to make travel easier for boats and ships. Natural riverbanks have been replaced with bricks and concrete. Many riverbanks are now lined with levees. These are human-made banks that are built high to contain rivers when they are flooding.

In 1993, the Mississippi River flooded. Over 50,000 homes and over 12,000 square miles (30,000 square kilometers) of farmland were flooded.

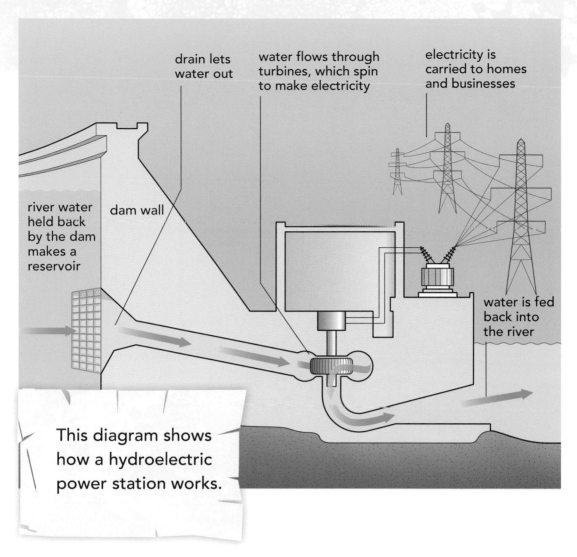

drain lets water out

water flows through turbines, which spin to make electricity

electricity is carried to homes and businesses

river water held back by the dam makes a reservoir

dam wall

water is fed back into the river

This diagram shows how a hydroelectric power station works.

All of these changes can have a bad effect on river **habitats**. When rivers lose their natural bends and curves, they lose areas of slow water, where many plants and animals live. Removing **sediment** means that there are fewer places for plants to grow and for tiny animals to live.

Dams

Huge **dams** have been built across some rivers. These create **reservoirs** behind the dams, used for **irrigation** and for piping to homes. Electricity can also be created at dams. Dams can affect river habitats by reducing the amount of water that flows downstream of the dam. Animals such as fish can be prevented from moving up and down rivers.

The Struggle to Survive

Many river **habitats** have changed as a result of human activity. Sometimes the different habitat has meant that different plants and animals can grow where they had not grown before. In the Murray-Darling river network in Australia, fish from other countries, such as the European carp, have been released. These fish can cope better than **native** fish with some of the changes to the river habitats.

Some native fish are no longer found in the Murray River in Australia.

The River Tyne in England was once so badly polluted that hardly any fish survived there. Now that the river is cleaner, salmon and trout are thriving. Many people enjoy fishing there.

Flowing clean

River habitats that have been damaged can recover if the **pollution** is stopped. This is because the flowing water keeps removing the pollution from the river.

A new fish

The Hudson River has some extremely polluted areas. Scientists have been surprised to find little fish called tomcod living there. These hardy fish have **adapted** to living with the chemicals in the river. Tomcod from other areas would not survive there.

25

River Restoration

River restoration is when people try to change a damaged river so that it becomes more like its natural self. This includes stopping or reducing the **pollution** and litter going into a river. It also includes taking away some of the structures on and around rivers. These structures might be **dams** or banks. Full restoration would involve putting bends and curves back into straightened rivers.

Creating habitats

River restoration means that rivers have lots of different areas—fast-flowing water, slow water, shallow areas, deep areas, muddy areas, stony areas. This means that lots of different kinds of plants and animals will be able to live there again.

This river is being restored.

Checking fish numbers is a good way of telling how clean a river is.

Ngakawau River, New Zealand

The Ngakawau River was polluted by waste from a nearby mine. Now, the waste goes into a large **reservoir** and the water is cleaned before it goes into the river. Now that the river is cleaner, there are more fish living in it.

The Future for River Habitats

An amazing range of plants and animals can be found in river **habitats**. The plants and animals living there have **adapted** to live under, on, and around the water.

However, many river habitats are now under threat. Human activity is changing rivers. The delicate balance of life in river habitats is being destroyed. Now that people know rivers need our help, we must use our knowledge to stop this damage.

How can you help?

You can do lots of things to help river habitats survive:

- Find out more about them—read books and research web sites.

- Join a conservation group that protects river species.

- Adopt an animal that lives in rivers.

- If you visit or use rivers, respect the environment and don't drop litter.

- Be water wise to help reduce the water taken from rivers.

These people are helping to clear litter from a river.

We need rivers!

Rivers are not just important for plants and animals. People need rivers. They provide us with water, food, and fun! Sailing, white-water rafting, fishing, and kayaking are just some of the many things that people can do on rivers.

Glossary

absorb take in or soak up

adapt change that helps a plant or animal survive in a particular place

algae very simple plants that mainly live in water

camouflage color or pattern used by an insect or animal to blend into the background

carbon dioxide gas that is found in air

channel long, narrow groove in the ground where water runs

dam barrier made to hold back water in a river

decomposer animal that eats dead and rotting plants and animals

energy power needed to move, grow, and live

erosion wearing away of Earth's surface

extinct no longer existing

fertilizer any substance added to soil to make crops grow better

food chain series of living things that provide food for each other

gill part of the body used by fish and other animals to breathe underwater

habitat place where a plant or animal lives

irrigation supplying water to land

larvae young form of many minibeasts, before they grow into adults

mammal warm-blooded animal that usually has fur or hair and drinks milk from its mother when it is young

native belonging to a particular country

nutrient substance that is taken in by an animal or plant to help it grow

oxygen gas that is found in air. All living things need oxygen to survive.

poison substance that can cause illness or death

pollution when a place is spoiled with litter or other harmful things

reservoir place where water is collected and stored

sediment tiny bits of solid material such as rock

sewage waste

water vapor water that has turned into a gas in the air

Find Out More

Books

Green, Jen. *Mighty Rivers* (Amazing Planet Earth). Mankato, Minn.: Smart Apple Media, 2010.

Johansson, Philip. *Lakes and Rivers: A Freshwater Web of Life* (Wonderful Water Biomes). Berkeley Heights, N.J.: Enslow Elementary, 2007.

Lynette, Rachel. *River Food Chains* (Protecting Food Chains). Chicago: Raintree, 2010.

Pyers, Greg. *Biodiversity of Rivers.* New York: Benchmark Books, 2011.

Internet Sites

Facthound offers a safe, fun way to find Internet sites related to this book. All of the sites on Facthound have been researched by our staff.

Here's all you do:

Visit *www.facthound.com*

Type in this code: 9781410946003

Index